How to Influence People the Right Way

By Jean Young

EXPERIENCE EVERYTHING PUBLISHING

Disclaimer

This document is geared towards providing exact and reliable information in regards to the topic and issue covered. The publication is sold with the idea that the publisher is not required to render accounting, officially permitted, or otherwise, qualified services. If advice is necessary, legal or professional, a practiced individual in the profession should be ordered.

- From a Declaration of Principles which was accepted and approved equally by a Committee of the American Bar Association and a Committee of Publishers and Associations:

In no way is it legal to reproduce, duplicate, or transmit any part of this document in either electronic means or in printed format. Recording of this publication is strictly prohibited and any storage of this document is not allowed unless with written permission from the publisher. All rights reserved.

The information provided herein is stated to be truthful and consistent, in that any liability, in terms of inattention or otherwise, by any usage or abuse of any policies, processes, or directions contained within is the solitary and utter responsibility of the recipient reader. Under no circumstances will any legal responsibility or blame be held against the publisher for any reparation, damages, or monetary loss due to the information herein, either directly or indirectly.

Respective authors hold all copyrights not held by the publisher.

The information herein is offered for informational purposes solely, and is universal as so. The presentation of the information is without contract or any type of guarantee assurance.

The trademarks that are used are without any consent, and the publication of the trademark is without permission or backing by the trademark owner. All trademarks and brands within this book are for clarifying purposes only and are the owned by the owners themselves, not affiliated with this document.

Introduction

The Most Influential People in the History

Nelson Mandela

Confucius

Aristotle

John F. Kennedy

Bill Gates

Chapter I: How to Start Influencing Other People

Reasons why others want to influence other people

First steps to get attention of other people

Show interest to others

Address the person who you talk to by their name

Participate actively in a discussion

Talk about the interests of the other people

Respect the opinion of what other people say or think

Engage with other groups and be as secure as possible

Chapter II: Establishing an Honest and Good Reputation

Admit mistakes as quickly as you realize you made one

Point out other's mistakes in positive manner

Show your expertise

Live your life in a clean way

Show your willingness to grow and learn

Introduction

People depend on other people in life, and it is important that everyone has someone they can admire who will, therefore, influence them to fulfill their own dreams. That is why people are often influenced by other people who have a leadership type personality. They want to be like the leader so they can be successful as well. The people looking up to this high up individual are very often open and willing to do what the leader tells them.

In this book, you will learn how you can be the person who influences people. You'll learn not only how to influence people for your own good, but to be of benefit to their lives as well. You'll learn methods of influencing other people in a good and positive manner that will help you both.

By reading this book you'll learn the most important things you can do to help and influence other people.

The Most Influential People in the History

The people below are examples of great influencers and their names have gone down in the history books as such. It is possible that some people have the ability to influence others because their minds focus on thinking positively. They always see things in a positive light. Others may say that they are gifted to have this opportunity to influence people but if you think about it, if another person can achieve this greatness, it means that you can do it as well.

Nelson Mandela

Nelson Mandela was a South African politician, anti-apartheid, and philanthropist who was the President of South Africa. He was South Africa's very 1st black chief executive. He focused on breaking the legacy of apartheid, tackled racism, and fostered racial reconciliation. He was loved by many because of being a philanthropist and also being the founder of democracy in South Africa.

Confucius

Confucius was the Chinese teacher, politician, editor, and philosopher in Chinese history. His ideas were the basis for the common principles now found in Chinese beliefs and traditions. He strongly influenced the respect to elders, family loyalty, and ancestors worship. He also came up with the saying and principle which is a Golden Rule: *"What you do not wish for yourself, do not do to others"*.

Aristotle

Aristotle became influential because of his contribution as the first genuine scientist in the history. His writings consist of many subjects such as biology, physics, zoology, ethics, logic, metaphysics, poetry, aesthetics, music, theater, rhetoric, government, politics and linguistics. He was Plato's student and, after the death of Plato, he became a great influencer to Byzantine scholars and Western Christian and Islamic theologians.

John F. Kennedy

John F. Kennedy became one of the most influential people in the history because of his contributions while he was the 35th president of the United States of America. Mainly his contribution was about bringing peace in the country and also removing the federal death sentence in District of Columbia. He was assassinated most likely because of his advocacy to help the Cuban people to be freed from the power of the Cuban leader Fidel Castro. However, there are still other theories surrounding his assassination that are being speculated.

Bill Gates

William Henry Gates III or Bill Gates is currently the richest man in the world. He is the chairman of Microsoft, an author, a philanthropist and the most influential because of his contribution to the programming world.

These are just some of the most influential people in the history and there are still many more. There was something that inspired them to be different and to help other people as well. That is something that we can duplicate from them, being different to achieve what we want in our life. What we need to do is influence other people and also learn from them, and for us to share the knowledge we have as well. Fulfilling your dreams or any achievement can be only done by you, but other people can help you along your journey. You just need to influence them to do so.

Chapter I: How to Start Influencing Other People

There are people that do not really have the ability to influence people and, if they do, they are afraid to use it for their own benefit and other's benefit as well. They are afraid to get negative feedback once they start speaking to other people.

Reasons why others want to influence other people

First of all it is good to intend to influence people because you want to be better and you want to help others to be better as well. Aiming to help others is not a usual trait of a person but probably is a gift because they have a good heart to help others.

Other reasons could be because other people want to share the good things that are happening to them. If they become wealthy because of what they did, they want other people to do it as well so they can be wealthy too.

In return for their kindness of influencing good in other people's lives, there is a positive outcome. Just remember the Law of Attraction, this is what they are teaching to other people.

The Law of Attraction means when you think positive only positive things happen. Instead of saying "I might be late at work" you can say "I know I can make it on time", and you surely will make it on time because of that positive thought.

In this chapter you will know the basic steps you can use to start influencing people. This helpful guide will not only help you get over your fear of actively influencing people but it will help you and others flourish due to your influence!

First steps to get attention of other people

We can not earn the trust of other people unless we do something that catches their attention. However, it would be odd if you immediately ask them something that is not right. Instead you can start with these steps:

1. Observe the people around you.

   You need to learn other people's way of communicating so if you want to join the conversation you would not offend them accidentally by using the wrong choice of words.

2. Think of a way to engage them in a conversation. You can ask them some simple questions that will catch their attention and can start the conversation. For example, if you are at an event you can ask them if they love the food and are they enjoying the party.

3. Be friendly, smile, and show your outgoing personality. Always be friendly and smile when you are speaking. Do not show them that you are overpowering them or you are higher than them. Always welcome them in the conversation with a smile.

Show interest to others

Being a good listener can show interest to others. People will confidently speak to others if they know that they are telling their story to a good listener. And being a good listener can gain trust from them. When they tell story make sure you ask questions that are on topic and make sure the questions aren't too personal, unless they seem willingly open to sharing a personal topic.

Address the person who you talk to by their name

After starting the conversation you need to make sure that you get the name of the person who you are talking to since addressing them by their name will make the conversation more personalized. By remembering their name they can see you are an interesting and interested individual who is paying attention to what they are saying.

Participate actively in a discussion

Building relationship with other people should be a two-way street. You should participate and let them participate as well. Think of it like you do not want to talk only to yourself. You should be encouraging them to engage to the conversation.

To encourage people to engage in the conversation, the topic should be interesting so that they can let themselves show you what they got. Make them feel that the conversation is meant for them as well. In this way you absolutely catch their attention and build good relationship to them. This could be also the start of helping them in a good way when you learn about their needs, dreams, and desires.

Talk about the interests of the other people

When you begin the conversation, you need to figure out the interests of the other person. Once they know that they can share something in the conversation, something about their interests, it will become an engaging conversation for the both of you. This will ensure the conversation won't end too quickly because will most likely have lots to talk about regarding their favourite subjects.

Respect the opinion of what other people say or think

It is important to respect other person's opinion regarding the topic. They might think differently than you do about a topic but if you happen to disagree, should say your reason the good way. You must state it in a way that they will not find offensive. You can state an example of your position but assure them that you will respect whatever they will comment about it and encourage them to give their opinion.

That way, they will not think that you disagree with them as a person if you happen to have different opinions and you show your respect to them.

Engage with other groups and be as secure as possible

This means that if you will are introduced by your friends to other groups of people, you should be also engaged in their conversation. Try to speak to them even you are just new. Do the same thing you would do if you were meeting an individual. Speak to them by knowing their interests, ask simple questions and listen to them when they start to speak. You can surely build relationships with them and know them more by showing interest in the conversation they already started within the group.

Chapter II: Establishing an Honest and Good Reputation

The next step you will need to do is establishing or building an honest reputation. Building a good reputation might not be easy to others but being honest could be the key in making a good one. This means being honest to people can be another step in gaining their trust as well.

The following can help you in establishing a good reputation.

Admit mistakes as quickly as you realize you made one

Never ignore the fact that you made a mistake and it is important to address it immediately. Admitting you made a mistake is the hardest thing to do and that is why other people admire people who own up to their mistakes. So if you made a mistake such as saying something bad about another person that was not true, immediately admit the mistake and do something to keep everyone's trust in you.

Point out other's mistakes in positive manner

In pointing out other people's mistakes, make sure that it is being told in positive way. It is still great to point out good things in a person's work but they will benefit even more if the mistake is being corrected.

In correcting other's mistake you must do it in positive way. You can do it not being hard on them like tapping their back and saying, "Good job on your work, there are just some small misses but overall it is great!" Make sure that you point out the good things they did on their job or work but make sure to let them know about their mistakes no matter how small or big it is. This is to ensure that they progress and do well in their job and is for their welfare as well.

Show your expertise

It is great if you can help others using your expertise! Your expertise can definitely be something that can help others. However, make sure that when you offer your expertise that is is in a way that you will remain approachable. Do not make them think that you "know it all" or in the end it may seem like you only know a little and are a bragard. It is best to be humble when showing your expertise.

Live your life in a clean way

If your aim is to win friends and influence other people, it is very important that you are living a clean life. You will gain respect from them and they might duplicate the way you are living your life so you want to be a positive influence. Examples include having a prestigious job, taking good care of look or appearance, eating healthy foods and staying fit, avoiding drugs and alcohol, respecting other people, following you dreams and participating the hobbies you love.

Show your willingness to grow and learn

Though you already have learned so much in life and they are all admirable, it is still significant to open your mind to learning new things. You can learn new things by travelling, engaging in more stimulating discussions, and being a person that will say 'yes' when being offered new learning experiences.

Chapter III: How to Guide Other People's Actions

Right after that you have gained trust and build a good and honest reputation to other people, it is still important that you continue to guide them. You must show them that you are still there no matter what. You must guide them on what they want to pursue and let them know that they can fulfill it with the power of their will.

Here are some tips that you can use to actively guide other people.

Take a good and friendly approach

Take a good and friendly approach if you want to influence other people. Think of a way that can make them immediately say yes to you to get their cooperation. An example of this is by asking questions like:

1. "Hey, I'm heading out to buy some food, would you like to come and join me?"
2. "I am a bit stressed lately, would you like to join me for a snack this afternoon and chat?"
3. "There is a great movie this week. I would like to watch it and to have some great company. Would you come and join me in watching it?"

Those were great examples of not just influencing other people but being friendly as well. This can be the start in guiding other people to think the way you think.

Sympathize with their opposing beliefs

Try to comprehend where they are coming from, those people that you are trying to influence. There are beliefs that might be opposing to what you believe, and respecting their opinions can build trust and respect from those people. Those people will appreciate you because of the respect they are getting when you are not disagreeing but sympathizing with their beliefs.

Influence people to change for the benefit of others

This may be a rare case but if you are able to influence others you can take advantage of your skills in influencing them to change them for the benefit of others. Other people are not that easy to be influenced in changing their character but if they can see that you have a point why they need to do it, there is possibility that they can be convinced. For example, if you see that one of the managers underneath you is always yelling at their subordinates, you can let them know that their subordinates will actually do better work with positive reinforcement. You can take an extra step by role playing with the manager to show them exactly how they should be talking to their subordinates. That way everyone involved wins. The manager gets better results and everyone else gets a better working environment.

Avoid being authoritative

To go along with the example in the last chapter, you can be a leader that does not need to shout when you need to give your orders. You can be authoritative in a way that you will not offend the people under you. Other people might lose their respect to you if they are hearing negative words or a negative way of giving your orders. Instead of saying "Get the papers for me!", say "Can you please get the papers for me?" It is a favor that you would greatly appreciate they do for you.

Praise the other people as recognition

Praise other people to recognize them for the good things they achieved. But be sure that when you give praise it should come from the heart. It should be the sincerest praise that they deserve. These people would be more motivated to do great things once they receive praise from their job. You can influence them more to keep up what they are doing and improve for their benefit as well.

Let other people share their ideas by giving clues and hints

Some people will not talk about their ideas unless you give hints about it. You may see that this person already knows what you think about this idea but because you want to influence them to share it, you can give a hint or a clue of what it is. For example, you may want to go out of town and you do not want to directly tell it to your partner, you can give a hint like you want to have a break from stressful work and you can ask your partner what is the best. You can provide a clue like a place that is great for a picnic or something that is nice to visit. Your partner would definitely suggest something that will come out from their own mouth after you gave them the clues.

Saving other people from embarrassment

No one can avoid being in an embarrassing situation that you do not want to happen every now and then. Embarrassing moments can actually be used to influence other people. This is by saving them from being noticed by other people during the embarrassing event. You can save a person from being too embarrassed by doing something for them. For example, if you see that someone is about to harass that person, you can intervene to stop the embarrassment or simply make the person aware of what is about to happen.

You can influence a person if they know that you are concerned to them and other people as well who may be experiencing the same situation as them.

Chapter IV: Other Helpful Tips to Learn How to Influence People

If you would like to win friends especially people that you may not think can be friendly as you are, you should think of something that can be a way to get closer to them. This is what they called the Benjamin Franklin effect. To explain it, this Benjamin Franklin effect is something you can use if there is someone you want to win. For example, there is a person who is not friendly to anyone and you want to influence them by being their friend. You might notice that the person is a bookworm. You can take advantage of that by asking them favor like borrowing the book they own that you also love. If they do not agree do not worry because that can be a start of the conversation. You can let them know that you are also a book lover and you love to read the same books that they read.

There are people that are able to not just influence positive people but also negative people as well. If you think that you want to influence negative people you can try to learn the tips below. But this may not guarantee changing negative people quickly because they have their own perception and it might take time for them to realize that they are being negative in their life. Here are some helpful ways to win negative people:

1. Do not argue or lead your conversation into an argument. You can throw questions and your point of view to them about a certain topic however, if it seems that the conversation is going around in circle and it is already leading to an argument then you need to be the first to stop. You may need to understand where they are coming from in the argument.

2. Negative people often complain more when they are doing tasks. That is why sometimes even when they are asking for help, they still sound like they are complaining. In this case to catch their attention you can throw them a question like, "Is there something that I can help with?" or maybe saying, "Are you alright?" This can surely make them feel that someone is of help even they did not realize were being a negative person.

3. Ignore the negativity you see in the person. If you notice that he or she is beginning to say or think negative thoughts, then swing it into a positive note. You can just say "okay" or "alright" whenever they speak negatively. Then if they become positive you should show them enthusiasm and interest. Do this step as often as possible, so they will realize that being positive pays off.

4. Always praise them for being positive. It is still believed that being positive can influence other people to become positive as well. So make sure to praise other people for being positive so they can continue it and eventually will reduce their trait of being negative.

5. If all of these tips fail, then it may be time to avoid them. Try to slowly avoid them and let them know about your intention of having good friends. You have your own life as well and it is not good to stay with them without anything good in return. You can just learn from them as experience.

It is a great achievement to influence negative people, but do not push yourself too hard if it is not working for many months or years. You need to think about yourself as well. There are so many people around the world that are waiting for your motivation and your skills in influencing them to do well in their lives. However, do not just throw away what you have learned from the negative people with whom you have interacted. You can still use your experiences with these negative people as a learning experience to influence other, more positive people.

Chapter V: Are you Still Afraid to Influence People?

It is just normal to be afraid in influencing people, because other people may think you are doing it for completely selfish reasons. But if you are sincere in your intentions you can not go wrong in influencing people.

Here are some questions that you can ask yourself. Write them down in a notebook as you go. Are you ready?

Here are the questions:

1. Why do you want to influence people? What are your intentions?
2. Is influencing people going to result in something positive for you and for the people you want to influence?
3. If you want to influence people, are you confident enough to support them all the way and do you have time for all of those people in your life?
4. Are you ready emotionally to take negative feedback from the people you want to influence?
5. In influencing people you may encounter those that will let you down, are you ready use all the tips you've found in this book or will you quickly give up?
6.

Take note of your answers before going to the next part where you can see the possible answers that might be the same as your answers. But remember there is no right and wrong response to the questions. This is just a test to see what you can do to influence people and how you will deal with the challenge.

If you are ready, you can take a look at the answers below now.

Here are the answers to the questions:

1. You might want to influence people because you want to share your talent and the things you are doing positively to better yourself. Your intentions to influence people are to show them that they can be even better than who they are now and have more in life.
2. If your intentions for influencing people are all good, it will be of great benefit to you and to them as well.

3. You should be confident enough to support the people you want to influence and have the time to do so because if not, you will not be able to successfully win them over. Remember that you should never stop supporting them and you should always be there whenever they need you.

4. Expect negative feedback from other people you want to influence and always be ready. You might get emotionally attached but that is just fine. Do not be too emotional but instead move on to the next person that you are sure you can influence with the good intentions you have if you must.

5. You cannot avoid those negative people and those who might let you down. So make sure you have those tactics that can reverse all the negative thoughts they have. You can tell them that you are just there as a concerned friend and letting you go can be regret on his part.

This is just a test to know what you can do to influence people and how successful you may be as an influencer. There are still other reasons, steps, tips, and how-to's that you can learn, but it will all come from within yourself. It is you who can make these things possible and in the end you will realize that you are already influencing people. Do not ignore the ability you have because it is only you who can use those skills to influence people.

Chapter VI: Have you learned something about this Book?

Hopefully you have learned some great tips in this book on how to influence people. It is wonderful if you have learned the ability to influence others and immediately can make them change to be a good or better person. People are not that eager to put their trust to someone because they fear they might be used for something that is not good for them. Some people are meticulous when it comes to choosing people to trust. You should always remember that so you know how to win people, how to gain their trust and how to keep their trust in you.

Once you gain the trust of other people, be sure to sincerely keep it. Always take care of them and support them until they can stand on their own shoes and beyond. There is no stopping when you are influencing people but you can let them be independent and assure them that you are always their number one fan while being positive.

Learning on how to influence people is a great and huge achievement and the people you have influenced will definitely be grateful for how you changed their lives. It should not be only because you want to take advantage of who they are and what you can gain from them, but you should have good and sincere intentions when influencing people. It is much better to see people achieving their dreams because of your influence than thinking about how to put them down for your own gain.

Conclusion

Throughout history there have been many influential people who were able to lead others in various countries and religions. There were also influential to their students because of their philosophy and teachings. They successfully influenced people because of their sincere intention to help others. However, there are also people in the history that used their influence to harm people which was not inspirational to others.

There are many reasons for influencing people but the main reason should be to help others to be the best version of themselve. Many people are wary of others who try to influence them because they think that they are just being used by the other person. They think that being influenced cannot do them any good but they should open up their mind to understand that "no man is an island" and as an influencer you can help them to do just that. There are people who will need you, and people you will need to fulfill all of your dreams or goals.

Do not be afraid to do what you can as an influencer. Yes, absolutely you also have the ability to influence people. You may just be afraid to try because you are scared to be rejected but even being rejected can help you become a better influencer.

Rejections are part of process of influencing people. You may not be successful as an influencer with some people but do not lose hope because there are millions of people in the world that you can influence and can ask for help as well. You just need to learn to observe them, talk to them nicely, listen to them, and also learn their interests in order to communicate with them effectively and positively. With all the tips you learned in this book you should have everything you need to go ahead and start influencing others for your benefit and their benefit as well.

www.ingramcontent.com/pod-product-compliance
Lightning Source LLC
Chambersburg PA
CBHW071812020426
42331CB00008B/2465